START-UP RELIGION

VISITING A GURDWARA

Kanwaljit Kaur-Singh and Ruth Nason

CHERRYTREE BOOKS

Distributed in the United States by
Cherrytree Books
1980 Lookout Drive
North Mankato, MN 56001

Library of Congress Cataloging-in-Publication Data
applied for

Conceived and produced by

White-Thomson Publishing Ltd.

Consultants: Jean Mead, Senior Lecturer in Religious
Education, School of Education, University of
Hertfordshire; Dr. Anne Punter, Partnership Tutor,
School of Education, University of Hertfordshire.
Designer: Carole Binding

Acknowledgments:
Special thanks to the following for their help and
involvement in the preparation of this book: the Sikh
Gurdwara South London (Southfields), Pavan Singh
Kooner, staff and children from Badshot Lea Village
Infants School.

Picture Acknowldgements:
All photographs by Chris Fairclough.

First Edition
9 8 7 6 5 4 3 2 1

First published in 2004 by
Evans Brothers Limited
2A Portman Mansions
Chiltern Street
London W1U 6NR
Copyright © Evans Brothers Limited 2004

Contents

Gurdwara Buildings

A **gurdwara** is a place where **Sikh** people go to **worship God.**

◀ **These Sikhs are arriving at their gurdwara. There is a Sikh symbol, called the khanda, on the gate.**

gurdwara   Sikh   worship   symbol

All gurdwara buildings have a flag outside called the Nishan Sahib. Many gurdwara buildings have a dome.

▼ The Nishan Sahib has the khanda on it.

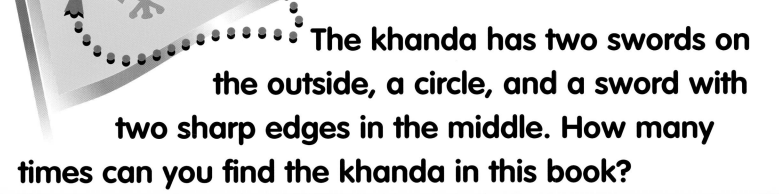

The khanda has two swords on the outside, a circle, and a sword with two sharp edges in the middle. How many times can you find the khanda in this book?

khanda   Nishan Sahib   dome

The Prayer Hall

▲ **This is the prayer hall in a gurdwara. The people are singing. To show respect, they wear no shoes and cover their heads. They sit facing the Sikh holy book, the Guru Granth Sahib. It is covered with beautiful cloths.**

prayer hall   respect   holy book

▼ When Sikhs go in to the prayer hall, they kneel in front of the Guru Granth Sahib and give some money.

▼ Then they bow to the Guru Granth Sahib. This shows respect for the words in it.

The money is used to help people in need and to look after the gurdwara.

Guru Granth Sahib   in need

Everyone is Equal

Sikhs believe that all people belong to one big family of God. In the gurdwara they show that everyone in the family is equal.

For example, women and men read from the Guru Granth Sahib and wave the fan called the chaur over it.

believe   equal   chaur

In the prayer hall, everyone sits on the floor (see page 6).

◀ Also, at the end of worship, everyone shares some special food called krah prashad.

▶ Then everyone goes to the dining hall for a meal called langar. Everyone helps to cook and serve the langar.

krah prashad   langar

A Kind of Uniform

Sikhs have a rule never to cut their hair. Uncut hair is like part of a uniform for Sikhs.

▶ Boys and men cover their long hair. Pavan wears a patka····· and his grandfather wears a turban.··

A steel bracelet is also part of the Sikh uniform. Its circle shape is a symbol of God because it has no beginning or end. Which other symbol has a circle? (See page 5.)

uncut hair   patka   turban

▼ You can see how Pavan's hair is tied on top of his head. This patka is a square of material with ties at each corner.

Sikh women and girls braid their long hair or tie it at the back of their neck. Many Sikh women wear Indian clothes. This means trousers, a dress, and a long scarf.

bracelet

A School Visit

▼ At the gurdwara, these visitors said "hello" in the Sikh way. What did they do with their hands?

► Inside, the visitors got ready to go into the prayer hall. Can you see two things they all had to do, to show respect?

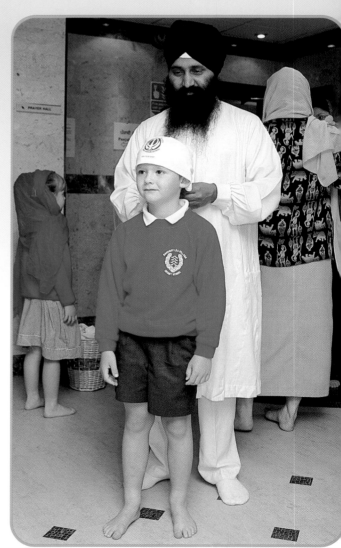

► On the way to the prayer hall, the visitors saw a picture of Guru Nanak. He started the Sikh religion, in Punjab in India. "Guru" means "wise teacher."

◄ Guru Nanak said, "There is only one God." How does he show this in this picture?

Guru Nanak   Punjab   Guru   13

The Guru Granth Sahib

Guru Nanak and nine other Sikh Gurus taught people about God and how to be good. The Gurus' words are written in the Guru Granth Sahib. Sikhs respect it like a real Guru.

▶ In the prayer hall the Guru Granth Sahib is kept on a stage under a canopy.

canopy

▲ Cloths called rumalas protect the Guru Granth Sahib.

▼ A chaur is waved over it. Chaurs were used in India to fan important people.

▶ On their visit, the children held a small chaur. It felt soft.

rumalas

Words and Symbols

▶ **The visitors listened to a reading from the Guru Granth Sahib. It is written in Punjabi.**

▼ **In Punjabi writing, the first words of the Guru Granth Sahib look like this.**

The words say:
There is one God.   God is Truth.   God is the Creator

Punjabi   Truth   Creator

There are several Sikh symbols on the carpet in front of the Guru Granth Sahib.

▶ One is the Ik Onkar. Can you tell what it means by looking at the Punjabi writing on page 16?

◀ A sword is a symbol of God's power. It reminds Sikhs that they should look after people who are not strong.

Ik Onkar   power   17

Singing and Music

When Sikhs worship in the prayer hall, they sing songs called shabads. The words are from the Guru Granth Sahib.

◀ The music for the singing is played on drums called tabla and a small organ called a harmonium.

▶ This book of shabads is called a gutka. What language is it in?

18

shabads   tabla   organ

The men who look after the prayer hall showed the children how to move the back of the harmonium to let in air, and how to tap the tabla.

harmonium   gutka   **19**

Langar

▶ The Sikhs at the gurdwara showed how they prepare the meal called langar (see page 9). They need big saucepans to cook for lots of people.

◀ The children made flat breads called chapattis. Can you see how they are cooked?

chapattis

Langar is always vegetarian. It is usually Indian food.

▲ The visitors were invited to try the food. Can you see the chapattis the children made? Making and sharing food was a friendly way to end the visit.

vegetarian

New words introduced in the text:

believe	equal	harmonium	Nishan Sahib	respect	turban
bracelet	gurdwara	holy book	organ	rumalas	uncut hair
canopy	Guru	Ik Onkar	patka	shabads	vegetarian
chapattis	Guru Granth	in need	power	Sikh	worship
chaur	Sahib	khanda	prayer hall	symbol	
Creator	Guru Nanak	krah prashad	Punjab	tabla	
dome	gutka	langar	Punjabi	Truth	

Background Information

Pages 4-5: Any place containing the *Guru Granth Sahib* (including a room at home) can be a gurdwara. In the United States, gurdwara buildings range from converted houses to specially built. All have the *Nishan* (identifying sign) *Sahib* (respected).

In the *khanda* the central sword is a symbol of justice and freedom. The circle represents God's infinite power. The outer swords remind Sikhs of their spiritual and secular responsibilities.

Pages 6-9: The main rooms in a gurdwara are the prayer hall and the *langar* (a kitchen/dining hall where food is served). *Langar* means both the hall and the food that is served there.

In the prayer hall a canopy hangs over the platform where the *Guru Granth Sahib* is placed on cushions and covered with cloths (*rumalas*). The *Guru Granth Sahib* contains the words of Guru Nanak (1469-1539), other Sikh Gurus and some Hindus and Muslims whose writings were in accord with Sikh teaching. In their treatment of the *Guru Granth Sahib;* Sikhs are not "worshiping the book" but revering the "Word" it reveals.

Sikhs believe in the oneness of God and the oneness of humanity and so Sikh services are open to anyone at all who wishes to pray to the one God. Before entering the prayer hall, everyone takes off their shoes and covers their head. Men and women often sit separately, but there is no rule about this.

There is no "holy day" in Sikhism, but most U.S. gurdwaras have a main service on either Saturday or Sunday. Worshippers sing *shabads* (hymns) from the *Guru Granth Sahib*. They stand up for a prayer called the *ardas* and then sit to hear a reading from the *Guru Granth Sahib*. The reader opens the book at random and reads the *hukam*–the Guru's guidance for the day. Finally, *krah prashad* (made from flour or semolina, sugar, water, and butter) is distributed to all the worshippers. The service is followed by *langar*.

Reflecting the belief in the oneness of humanity, women and men can read from the *Guru Granth Sahib* and take equal part in leading services and in cooking and serving the *langar*.

Pages 10-11: Uncut hair (*kes*) and a steel bracelet (*kara*) are two of the "five Ks,", which can be called the "uniform" of Sikhs. The wearing of the five Ks was started by the tenth Sikh Guru, Guru Gobind Singh, who in 1699 organized the Sikh community (called the *Khalsa*) in Punjab. These symbols signify a commitment to the *Khalsa*.

The religion requires Sikhs to wear the five Ks, but there are some who don't and still identify themselves as Sikhs.

Kes is a symbol of commitment to God's will. As well as God's infinite power, the *kara* symbolizes unity and strength.

Parents and Teachers

The other three Ks are the *kanga* (a wooden comb worn in the hair and a symbol of cleanliness), *kachh* (undershorts, a reminder of sexual purity and self-control), and *kirpan* (a sword, to symbolize God's power and the Sikh's duty to defend the weak; many Sikhs wear or carry a small symbolic sword).

Sikh men are usually recognisable by their turbans and boys by their *patka*. Apart from this, many Sikh men in the United Kingdom wear Western dress, although some wear traditional Indian long, loose shirt and trousers. Many women wear Punjabi suits.

Pages 12-13: The Punjabi greeting is "*Sat Sri Akal,*" meaning "The True God is immortal."

Visitors to a gurdwara should try to take head coverings with them, although the gurdwara will provide these if necessary.

Guru Nanak started the Sikh religion in Punjab in 1499. It was a time of conflict between Hindus and Muslims and Guru Nanak's message was "There is neither Hindu nor Muslim, only God's path. I shall follow God's path."

Pages 14-15: Traditionally the *chaur* is made from yak's hair.

Pages 16-17: The *Guru Granth Sahib* is written in the Gurmukhi script (the script in which Punjabi is written) and all copies have 1,430 pages. The *Ik Onkar* is the Gurmukhi script for "There is only one God."

Pages 18-19: The whole of the *Guru Granth Sahib* is written in *shabads* (verses). These are set to *ragas* (musical notations) for singing. Some gurdwaras employ professional musicians called *ragees* to lead the singing of *shabads* at services.

Pages 20-21: The importance of hospitality in Sikhism means that visitors to the gurdwara are usually offered food. Be well prepared, knowing what individual children can and will eat. For Sikhs, preparing and serving food in the *langar* are part of their *sewa* (service: giving time, money, and skills to help others and taking pleasure in doing this). The *langar* food is vegetarian so that everyone can eat it. The *chapattis* were made with flour and water and a little oil, and cooked on a griddle.

Recommended Resources

BOOKS

Kaur-Singh, K. *My Sikh Faith* (Big Book). London: Evans, 1999.

Kaur-Singh, K. *Sikh Gurdwara*. London: A & C Black, 2000.

WEB SITES

www.cyber-link.net/history.htm
www.gurdwara.us
www.sikhkids.com

Suggested Activities

■ Visit a local gurdwara or use a virtual visit. Discuss how it made the children feel.

■ Show a video clip of a Sikh service or invite a Sikh to talk about a service.

■ Discuss mealtimes, who you share them with, and what it means to eat together. List jobs involved in preparing a meal. What equipment and amounts of food are needed to prepare a meal for a very large number?

■ Can children recognize Sikhs in pictures? Discuss why many Sikhs think it is important to wear their religious uniform. Link to school uniform and talk about the importance of being part of a community. Also consider how people are treated if their appearance makes them "stand out."

■ Tell some stories about Guru Nanak and about Guru Gobind Singh and the beginning of the *Khalsa*.

■ The Sikh Gurus and the *Guru Granth Sahib* teach Sikhs how to lead a good life. Talk about the qualities of teachers.

■ Discuss special books and how you look after them.

■ Listen to a tape of *shabads* and pick out the sounds of the harmoniums and *tabla*.

Index